Structural Social Work

in Action

Structural Social Work

in Action

Examples from Practice

Edited by

STEVEN F. HICK, HEATHER I. PETERS, TAMMY CORNER, and TRACY LONDON

Canadian Scholars' Press Inc.

Toronto

Published by
Canadian Scholars' Press Inc.
425 Adelaide Street West, Suite 200
Toronto, Ontario
M5V 3C1

www.cspi.org

Canadian Scholars' Press Inc. gratefully acknowledges financial support for our publishing activities from the Government of Canada through the Book Publishing Industry Development Program (BPIDP) and the Government of Ontario through the Ontario Book Publishing Tax Credit Program.

The royalties from this book will be donated to support the human rights work of the International Federation of Social Workers (IFSW).

Library and Archives Canada Cataloguing in Publication

Structural social work in action : examples from practice / edited by Steven F. Hick ... [et al.].

Includes bibliographical references.
ISBN 978-1-55130-364-2

1. Social service. 2. Social case work. I. Hick, Steven F

HV40.S845 2009   361.3'2   C2009-904533-8

Cover design, interior design, and layout: Susan MacGregor/Digital Zone

MIX
Paper from
responsible sources
FSC® C004071

Printed and bound in Canada